The Contest

Carmel Reilly

Christina Miesen

Australia • Brazil • Japan • Korea • Mexico • Singapore • Spain • United Kingdom • United States

The Contest

Fast Forward
Silver Level 23

Text: Carmel Reilly
Illustrations: Christina Miesen
Editor: Johanna Rohan
Design: Vonda Pestana
Series design: James Lowe
Production controller: Seona Galbally
Audio recordings: Juliet Hill, Picture Start
Spoken by: Matthew King and Abbe Holmes
Reprint: Siew Han Ong

ISBN 978 0 17 012697 7
ISBN 978 0 17 012693 9 (set)

Cengage Learning Australia
Level 7, 80 Dorcas Street
South Melbourne, Victoria Australia 3205
Phone: 1300 790 853

Cengage Learning New Zealand
Unit 4B Rosedale Office Park
331 Rosedale Road, Albany, North Shore NZ 0632
Phone: 0508 635 766

For learning solutions, visit cengage.com.au

Printed in Australia by Ligare Pty Ltd
6 7 8 9 10 11 12 21 20 19 18 17

Evaluated in independent research by staff from the Department of Language, Literacy and Arts Education at the University of Melbourne.

The Contest

Carmel Reilly
Christina Miesen

ARACHNE WAS A TALENTED YOUNG SPINNER AND WEAVER. SHE HAD LEARNED ALL SHE KNEW FROM HER TEACHER ATHENA, THE GREEK GODDESS OF ARTS AND CRAFTS.

ARACHNE MADE THE MOST WONDERFUL FABRICS AND TAPESTRIES THAT WERE NOT ONLY BEAUTIFUL, BUT WERE USED LIKE PAINTINGS, TO TELL STORIES.

UNHAPPILY FOR HER, SHE WAS PROUD AND STUBBORN, AND IT WAS ONLY A MATTER OF TIME BEFORE SHE, AND THE POWERFUL, AND EQUALLY PROUD AND STUBBORN ATHENA, CLASHED.

THAT'S LOVELY WORK,
MY DEAR.
YES, I AM PLEASED WITH IT. I THINK IT'S THE BEST THING THAT'S EVER BEEN DONE IN THIS WORKSHOP.
WHAT?
BETTER THAN THE GODDESS ATHENA'S WORK?

YES, LOOK AT THIS AND TELL ME IT'S NOT BETTER THAN ATHENA'S WORK.
IT'S NOT A GOOD IDEA TO BOAST THAT YOU ARE BETTER THAN A GODDESS.
AFTER ALL, SHE DID TEACH YOU EVERYTHING YOU KNOW.
I'M NOT BOASTING! I'M TELLING THE TRUTH. I TAUGHT MYSELF MOST OF THIS. SEE HOW ORIGINAL MY WORK IS?
ATHENA HAS NEVER DONE ANYTHING LIKE THIS. IF WE HAD A CONTEST NOW, I WOULD WIN.

Running Words 214

AS EVERYTHING SETTLED AGAIN,
ARACHNE LOOKED UP
TO SEE THAT THE OLD WOMAN
HAD DISAPPEARED.
IN HER PLACE STOOD THE GODDESS, ATHENA,
WHO STARED ANGRILY DOWN AT ARACHNE.
SO, YOU THINK YOUR WORK
IS BETTER THAN MINE.
YOU THINK THAT YOU,
A SIMPLE HUMAN,
ARE BETTER THAN ME, A GODDESS!
OH!

I HAVE BECOME A BETTER WEAVER THAN YOU, MY TEACHER. LOOK AT MY BEAUTIFUL WORK! LOOK! YOU CAN'T DENY IT!
I'M SURE THAT MOST PEOPLE WOULD NOT AGREE.
HA! YOU HAVE NO IDEA.

I'M NOT AFRAID OF ATHENA. SHE WANTS ME TO BE AFRAID, BUT I WON'T PLAY HER GAME.
I'M SO SICK OF GODS THINKING THEY CAN BOSS HUMANS AROUND.
WELL, LET'S HAVE A CONTEST! YOU'LL SEE THEN THAT PEOPLE THINK I'M BETTER THAN YOU ARE.
I WILL TAKE UP YOUR CHALLENGE. BUT REMEMBER, NO ONE EVER BEATS A GODDESS, ARACHNE.
NO ONE.

ARACHNE DECIDED TO WEAVE A HUGE TAPESTRY THAT WOULD SHOW THE STORIES OF GODS AND HUMANS SINCE THE BEGINNING OF TIME.

SOON THEY WILL ALL SEE HOW GOOD I AM.

ARACHNE WANTED EVERYONE TO SEE HOW HER WEAVING COULD MAKE THE SCENES COME ALIVE.

ATHENA, HOWEVER, HAD DECIDED ON SOMETHING QUITE DIFFERENT FOR HER TAPESTRY. AT THE TIME, SHE WAS ALSO IN COMPETITION WITH POSEIDON, ANOTHER GREEK GOD, TO BECOME THE RULING GOD OF THE CITY. SHE DECIDED TO SHOW IN HER TAPESTRY HOW SHE WAS GOING TO WIN THAT COMPETITION.

THEY WILL SEE HOW POWERFUL I AM.
THEY WILL KNOW THAT I AM THE RIGHT GOD TO RULE THIS CITY.
LOOK AT HER FINE WORK.
I LIKE HER CONFIDENCE. I'M GOING TO VOTE FOR HER.
ME, TOO.

MONTHS LATER ...
THIS IS MY BEST PIECE EVER.
WONDERFUL, ATHENA!
WE VOTE FOR YOU, ATHENA, GODDESS OF OUR CITY.
LET'S CALL OUR CITY ATHENS IN HER HONOUR!
YES! ATHENS, FOR ATHENA.

ATHENA ASKED ARACHNE TO HER HOME TO LOOK AT HER TAPESTRY.
SO, WHAT DO YOU THINK, ARACHNE?
IT'S LOVELY ...
BUT NOT AS LOVELY AS MINE.
HA! JUST AS I WON AGAINST POSEIDON, I WILL WIN AGAINST YOU, TOO.

WHEN ARACHNE RETURNED TO THE WORKSHOP, SHE WAS DETERMINED TO DO EVEN BETTER WITH HER WORK.

LET'S SEE NOW WHO PEOPLE WILL VOTE FOR. ME WITH MY BEAUTIFUL WORK AND MY TRUE STORY, OR HER ...
SO, WHOSE IS BEST?
ARACHNE'S WORK IS GOOD.
BUT, SO IS YOURS, ATHENA.
WE CAN'T DECIDE.
LEAVE US. WE NEED TO SPEAK TO EACH OTHER ALONE!

MY WORK IS BEST.
YOU HAVE INSULTED THE GODS WITH THIS WORK!!
WHAT?

YOU'RE JUST JEALOUS!
YOU WANT AN EXCUSE TO SAY
IT'S NOT AS GOOD AS YOURS.
NO! NO! NO!

YOU'VE DESTROYED MY BEAUTIFUL TAPESTRY. AND, I CAN SEE THAT YOU'RE GOING TO DESTROY MY LIFE!
IF YOU LOVE WEAVING THAT MUCH, I WILL MAKE YOU INTO A CREATURE WHO DOES NOTHING BUT SPIN AND WEAVE. AND, YOUR CHILDREN AND THEIR CHILDREN WILL ALL DO THE SAME! FOREVER AND EVER!

NO! NO!
WHAT ARE YOU DOING TO ME?

TODAY, THE CHILDREN OF ARACHNE
CAN BE FOUND EVERYWHERE –
IN THE CORNERS OF WINDOWS,
AND IN THE BRANCHES OF TREES.
THEY KEEP FAR AWAY FROM OTHER CREATURES.
INSTEAD, THEY SPEND THEIR TIME SPINNING
THE FINEST OF THREADS
AND WEAVING THE MOST BEAUTIFUL
AND DELICATE OF MATERIALS –
WEBS TO CATCH THEIR PREY.